I0210983

EMBODIED

poems by

Karen Klein

Finishing Line Press
Georgetown, Kentucky

EMBODIED

Publisher: Leah Huete de Maines
Editor: Christen Kincaid
Cover Art: Karen Klein
Author Photo: Isvel Bello
Cover Design: Elizabeth Maines McCleavy

Order online: www.finishinglinepress.com
also available on amazon.com

Author inquiries and mail orders:
Finishing Line Press
PO Box 1626
Georgetown, Kentucky 40324
USA

Contents

.

The Facts of Life

that last day I went first
at the fence top
lifting one leg to jump over
my summery dress slipped up   exposing
little girl underpants' crotch
below me I heard the boys laughing
Paul and Ralph   my best friends
until we were seven

stealing apples from the neighbors' back yard
was our favorite game
we had to climb over a metal fence
taller than we were
empty spaces between wires fit our kid shoes

at the top   puzzled   hurt
jumped down to the other side
the fence forever between us
still hearing their laughter
not with me
at me

Clitoris

You've never heard that word spoken, have you?
my analyst asks. *No,* I answer, *just read it.*

never heard it   saw it
mother in the tub   outstretched
her hand guiding the washcloth
separates her legs
at the cleft   a strange protuberance
smaller   thinner than a finger
there

nine year old me   perched on the tub's rim
always wants to be near her   my own Ingrid Bergman
curious about what I see   scared by it
what's that?
silence   then   *nothing*
still air between us
then   *nevermind*   shuts it up
forever   never mentioned   no words

no names   for what I saw
for what I found   I had
like her   not like hers
my favorite shorts   almost a short skirt
the pant legs opening   so wide
a hand could easily slip in
and his did

our summer helper's boyfriend
in the old rocker on the back porch
his invitation   *come sit on my lap*
we sat   my back to his chest
his hand gently sliding under the elastic
of my panties   massaging me
where   mother said no one
not even me
should ever touch

I bet this feels good
his voice startles me into jumping off
run   find mother   tell her
a man touched me   'down there'
my secret I kept to myself
never told
it felt good

He tackles me.
I feel his body fall on mine
pinning me
to the dry earth. His arms
and hands pincer grips on my wrists
grinding them harsher and more harsh
into the dirt.

He wants to kiss her.

   I was 10.
   He was 10   maybe 11.

On recess we go out to look for horses
a small unchaperoned group of Fifth Graders
the oldest class at the homelike private school
surrounded by fields.

Their chant starts.
He wants to kiss her.

His woodpecker attempts at kisses
trying to land on my lips
to catch them from my moving face
my head turning side to side and back again
my frantic   silent   gesture...

He wants to kiss her.

Their laughter, urging him on.

Sensing threat, I run
back to the safety
of the school buildings...
grabbed
flung on my back.

They witness.

Capture complete, he gets off.

In Mom's car on the way home,
my sobbing demands *go tomorrow*
tell the headmaster
I didn't ask for it.
Not my fault.

* "Got a crush on you, Sweetie Pie" music and words, George and Ira Gershwin, 1930

Stains

at thirteen I got the mumps
swollen and sick   blood
on the toilet paper
scared this strange infection permeated
my entire body   told mom

a large linen closet
in which anything could be tucked away
remain secret
from its depth she brought out a box
bulky white pads   an elastic belt for my waist
two straps one for front
the other for back
at each end metal hooks
to secure pad's thinner ends
a trough for blood under my genitals
to wear over
my under
pants

you have your sick time she told me
never tell your father
I never did

coming home after a high school movie date
we two hung out in the kitchen
my steady boyfriend recited a dirty song
his brother in the navy told him
my summer dress full   flowy   a pale green
I turned away
his spontaneous nervous laugh
brought me round
the taboo stain   the period leak
embarrassing me into awkward
both pretended it wasn't there

never acknowledged
female power
to bleed without a wound
its forbidden appearance
my shame

Voltage

the kiss   long hard intense
bringing me somewhere
too new

been kissed before
but never reacted
so charged

college freshman at seventeen
I'm dating a senior
who has a car

protracted kiss made me
tense with pleasure's need
to pinch, claw, grasp, bite

and I did

our moist mouths
more moist
with a thin tincture

opening his bleeding lower lip
he screamed   *what are you
a crocodile*

we still dated
avoiding electricity
reverberations linger

in his roommates
teasing greeting
Hiya Croc

that's the way we do it uh-huh, uh-huh

desperate   a virgin   New York City roommates happily
sexually active   I need to get laid

all the teenage years of not letting him get to Third Base
giving just enough   but not enough enough……..

the balancing act between getting a reputation
known either as   frigid   or   fuckable

at twenty-one   deliberately   surrender my virginity
to another neophyte   my best friend

the earth didn't move   but my vagina
crossed the Rubicon

'so, dear reader, I married him'   that's what we did
we girls of the 1950's

we had sex and married the man
we had sex with

a few of us went to the altar
virginally white   or said we were   while others

not so cautious as I   had to get married
then spent years   fudging their marriage date

to their children   who always suspected they were
the unintended cause   of an unwanted union

Onset

for j.h.k. b.11/18/1961

I.

room's cold brightness
on all sides of me interns   residents—
all male— a teaching hospital

pressure to push accelerates pain
reach out to one   pleading
hold my hand

his sudden surprised response *why?*
OB doctor commands *just do it*
she likes to hold hands

all childbirth is natural
unmedicated childbirth brutal
first time ever use

of my vagina as a birth canal
that moment in the cold delivery room
my life irrevocably changed

II.

no crib   our too small apartment
on the dresser top a bassinette
courtesy of Best&Co. layette provider

mostly alone, I stand and watch her
sleeping on her back   swaddled
as the hospital nurse taught me

the size of one of my childhood dolls
the biggest one Agnes
my mother's name

but not a doll
she's breathing
what have I done

how do I learn
to care for
what I have done

Hiker

for m.w.k. b.5/8/1964

she would only sleep
in the crib with slats
open to the air
                to the light
freedom's child

eager to escape   my second daughter
tore out   her skin still blue til breath entered
Adonai's spirit   *ruah*
blue blushed to creamy   I watched
life enter

confinement resister at nine months
hoisting herself over crib's slat barrier
slid to floor   to closed door   my nightly check
unable to open   blocked by her body
slumbrous doorstop

skier   hitch-hiker
off to summer camp age nine
my helpless parenting   arms not stretchy enough
to hold her independence
only my heart

slate ocean
the young kestrel puts one leg
then the other into its wetness
eases onto its surface
swims out

The Violent Birth of Stars

for e.a.k. b.5/13/1967

Because I forgot
with the first two,
I kept a journal
on yours.

Pain has no memory,
only the memory
of a memory
infinitely receding
till it returns in the body,
sharp, intimate,
as if it had never happened,
a new thing.

To keep ahead of it
I panted, blew, gulped
swallowed the air
that would drive you out
between my helplessly
trembling legs.

I couldn't outrun it.
Knees up, heels down,
sliding along the sheets
up-down, up-down
head side-to-side-
my whole body
a rhythmic mantra
against my belly's rising
into that firm ridge
an elephant could stand on.

When the time came,
I remembered from the other two
that my body did not split
groin to skull,

so it was safe to push
as you tore your way
into the air.

Later, in the recovery room
I consider getting pregnant again.
After giving birth,
everything is anticlimactic.

Mothering

water in the hollow
of the smooth stone
sleeps and smiles

bending over the bassinet
in wonder and terror
swaddled sleeper
make sure she breathes

towhead on my lap
wrapping a towel
around a new toddler
wet from the sprinkler

on the apricot silk dress
covering my nipples
the slow spreading stain
of breast milk for the baby

the peace of sucking
the water in the stone

grammar

I.

not punctuation   not a black dot
signifying the end of a sentence or multiple ellipses

but a duration beginning   timer set   end
this periodicity does not appear on your desktop or

corporate calendar   presence felt   marking time
in female bodies monthly measurement

tidal blood flow   set by our reproductive fate
the moon is our model   our shining guide   our jailer

private yet universal meanings for late   missed
at sixteen I have a boyfriend   am late and scared

telling mom leads to the gynecologist's office
where I bleed

mom and my surprised relief   she says
if you had been   it would have killed your father

What does my father have to do with it?

II.

years marked with lunar memories
gut cramps double over   moods circle the moon and spin

plans made unmade   welcome times when missed
a new future   ungrammatical times when missed
what future

I was mother of three   then late
raging   waiting   praying   waiting

wanting to reject   the lunar contract
unbidden   at birth

not mine   to reject or accept
all the eggs   already in my infant ovaries

my powerlessness   my moonbody's power
which will eventually cease

How then will my body measure time's flow?

Nothing but trouble

I

my 40th birthday
I want another baby
missed a month   gynecologist verdict
no fetus no possible life no unborn child

just multiple twisted fibrous muscle
tumors within wrapping my uterus
growths made by my own body but not
a new birth   an invasion of my body

by my body   possibly dangerous
next step   surgical menopause
how did my body know to alert me
to urge one more try

II

new scar   bikini cut
cross pubis   pelvic bone to pelvic bone
first step post surgery
felt my gut fall out

new awareness   new liberation
no more anxious waiting no more fears
no wonder guys like sex
no life changing consequences

III

at 56 my body's dreamsignal
ultrasound confirms
pre-cancerous ovarian cyst
bikini cut reopened restitched

painful recovery confirms
longtime now longgone
OB's prediction
after 40 they're nothing but trouble

new questions
from well-meaning   curious friends
do you still feel you are
a woman?

Song

chalk in my mouth
somewhere in my belly
shriveled fallopians
my uterus and ovaries
long gone to the knife
like my daughter's
leftover eggs
to the refuse cans
medical waste

orange berries
of my neighbor's bittersweet
bright in the October sun
shiny, smooth, hard globes
inedible

Wellfleet

down the beach a crowd of adolescent
boys and girls   their laughter cascades
over us late middle-age moms on a 'girls weekend'
they yell, tease, chase each other in
and out of the water   energized for pleasure

my body's sudden   unsought   genital awareness
back with the gang at Marv's lake cottage
Minnesota summer   my boyfriend Ronnie
there with us   tonight in his car
I'll play sex chess

will I be captured
can I play
—I sure want to—
and not lose the thing
I'm most valued for

not a memory   a forever presence
bred in my flesh and female bones
the deliciousness of my desire
the danger of disgrace
its terrible consequences

Why buy the cow when you can get the milk for free?

I flash on that day in Wellfleet
years later   driving in urban traffic
stalled at the lights
two males   easy in their early manhood skin
thread deftly through the cars

their bare   muscular arms
T-shirts tight across full chests
sleeves rolled way up   hold a cigarette pack
why didn't I just fuck them all
when I still could

Ineffable

is   not sayable
meaning   poetry's tongue
silenced   but the tongue
begins   moistening lips

reaching into mystery
the other's   mouth
talking   without sound
darting dance   light touch here

there   smooth rim circling
rubbing along   sharp edge of bite
lips swell   to fasten
in pas de deux   partnering

unbidden   grace comes
flooding presence   certainty of a god
the giving over to that power
volitionless   wet

Lust in the aged

Think of Chaucer's ugly Merchant
crowing the morning after his wedding night,
—bride beside him inappropriately young—
the slack skin around his scrawny neck shaking,
wattles of a clichéd dirty old man.

But what of dirty old women? More shameful,
just like Chaucer's Wife of Bath, old and obese,
confessing that she still has a 'coltes tooth',
meaning her unabated appetite for sex.
Mine, too, but imagine the personal ad:

eightysomething, pendulous breasts, good legs,
loves to go dancing, Dvorak chamber music,
seeks man who has made sure he's still capable
of sexual activity as the ads
to repair erectile dysfunction caution.

But wait; sexual activity covers
a lot of orifices and practices.
I'd like to specify 'the old in and out'
aware, however, that doing so narrows
the applicant pool considerably.

In the mail, a package from a woman friend,
containing a shape carved simply out of wood,
an abstract, quite possibly figurative,
the head with hair styled almost in a page-boy,
its body a cylindrical six inches.

The printed tag around its neck says 'wise soul'.
I call her to say thanks for the wise woman.
I know I need wisdom, but I'm not there yet.
She, laughingly, replies, *that's not a woman,
it's a penis;* its erection guaranteed.

Now I wonder if stiffness is the only thing I need.

10,000 Steps per day

not walkin' to New Orleans
nor out at midnight looking for you
all the almost old   the newly old
even the old old   carved walking sticks
canes   long unused ski poles retrieved
no Circean promise of immortality
just the precise prescription: ambulate
all the old will stay forever old
but not look old

full circle from first loopy steps
crib to 10, 000 daily   like babies now
X and Y issues long dealt with
perhaps a leftover prostate   a prolapsed uterus
only diaper secrets reveal sex
no longer procreative   rarely recreative
always eliminative
sharing symptoms and surgeries
we collectors of specialists

difference ages out   blurs
memory elides   mating cruelties
rueful compassion heals marital rages
the Riddle of the Sphinx defines
our species   homo sapiens
we bi-pedal mammals
who walk on four feet at dawn
two at noon
three at night

Lines

Paul Klee went for a walk with one
Johnny Cash walked the line
commands: get in line   line up
you're out of line

Fishing lines   lines of demarcation
zigzag   diagonal perpendicular
equatorial   clef lines
lineups   headlines

Women know the most significant
lines are worn on our skin
"furrowed brow" "crow's feet" "marionettes"
"wrinkles" as if we were covered in chintz

Facial lines make mirrors enemies
but the word line is innocent of its modifiers
So pick whichever line you want
for me   I prefer line of verse

ACKNOWLEDGMENTS

The author would like to thank the editors of the following journals, where these poems first appeared.

Nina Rubenstein Alonso, editor and publisher of *Constellations*:
  that's the way we do it, uh-huh, uh-huh, Vol.12, Fall 2022
  The Facts of Life, and *Lust in the Aged,* Vol.13, Fall 2023
  Voltage, Vol. 14, Fall 2024

Doug Holder, publisher; Harris Gardner, poetry editor, *Ibbetson Street*
  Onset, #53
  Lines, #54

Bagel Bards Anthology #15, editor Wendell Smith
  Nothing But Trouble
  10, 000 Steps per day

Capewomenonline,net/poetry-page-readers-poetry-page
  Violent Birth of Stars

The author would also like to thank Steve Glines, editor and publisher of *Wilderness House Literary Review* and Zvi Sesling, editor and publisher of *Muddy River Literary Review* for publishing my poems that are not included in Embodied due to different subject matter, but were published during the same time period.

APPRECIATION

As poet, I am deeply indebted to these workshops, their leaders, and most recent fellow participants:

Tom Daley, Mondays, 5:30-7:30pm
with Brian Delaney, Eileen Simon, Eva Maria Basinska, Gunilla Kester, Margaret Bryant, Mary Wisbach

Judson Evans, Fridays, 10:30am-noon
with Ruth Hoberman, Samanthe Sheffer

After 37 years in the English and American Literature Department and the first faculty member of that department to teach a course on women writers in 1970-71, and Co-Director, then Director of the Undergraduate Humanities Program at Brandeis University in Waltham, MA, **Karen Klein** retired in 2001 as Associate Professor Emerita. She turned her attention to her creative activities: first studying and performing contemporary modern dance. As a young woman in the late 1950's and early 1960's, she was a student of Martha Graham in New York City and the Jose Limon Company at the Connecticut School of the Dance. She continued her studies of dance and performed in the Boston area with Across the Ages Dance for eight seasons and with Prometheus Elders from 2005 to 2019. Adding to her dance training, in the mid-1990's, Klein began a haiku/senryu writing practice at least one poem per day and publishing in major haiku journals, e.g. Modern Haiku, Frogpond. Adding contemporary lyric poems to her creative activity, she has published frequently in these print journals: Constellations, Ibbetson Street, and online in Wilderness House Literary Review and Muddy River Literary Review. She started a poetry/dance collective, teXtmoVes with performances in the greater Boston area and on Cape Cod from 2016 until 2023. Her first full-length poetry book, *This Close* (Ibbetson Street Press, Somerville, MA, 2022) and her first chapbook, *Embodied* (Finishing Line Press, Georgetown, Kentucky, 2025). She is the co-author with linocut artist, Scott Ponemone, *Circularity* (BookArt, ca.Montreal, Canada,2025).

She is working on a third MS, *1324 Third Avenue South* about growing up in Fargo, North Dakota from 1936-1954 when she came to Cambridge, MA for college. She has remained an East Coast resident, living in Manhattan, New York; Fort Walton Beach, Florida; Brookline and Wayland, MA, and settled in Cambridge, MA.